Jennifer Lopez

She can dance. She can sing. She is a smart businesswoman. She is beautiful and she is Hollywood's number one *Latina*★ movie star. But the story of Jennifer Lopez starts in New York.

Young Jennifer

It is July 24, 1970—a hot summer day in the Bronx, New York. A lot of Puerto Rican people live here and they are not all happy. But it is a good day for David and Guadalupe Lopez and their daughters Lynda and Leslie. They are happy because they have a new little girl in the family. They call her Jennifer.

Jennifer is beautiful and interesting. From four years old she performs for the family. Sometimes she is a singer. Sometimes she is a dancer or a movie star. She loves the movie *West Side Story*. She watches it one hundred times. In *West Side Story*, Rita Moreno plays Anita. For Jennifer, Rita is America's number one actress and dancer. "I'd like to be her," Jennifer thinks.

At five, Jennifer goes to a school of theater and dance. In a short time, she can sing, act, and dance very well.

"But is this important?" David and Guadalupe ask. They have good jobs. They want to see Jennifer in a good job, too. For this, schoolwork is very important.

★ *Latina*: In Latin American countries, people talk in Spanish or Portuguese. A *Latina* is a Latin woman.

Jennifer (left) in Living Color

Jennifer the Dancer

In 1975, Jennifer goes to the Holy Family Catholic School in New York. It is a good school and she is a good student. But in 1983, the problems start. Now schoolwork is not very important to Jennifer. She wants to be a performer.

One day in 1988, she says, "I want to stop going to school." David and Guadalupe are angry. Jennifer is angry with them, too. She walks out of the house.

Jennifer lives in her dance school for a short time. Then she moves into an apartment in Manhattan with some friends. She dances in the school every day. She works well. Then she starts to look for a job.

"This is going to take a long time," Jennifer thinks.

She is wrong. First, she gets a job in the theater show *Golden Musicals of Broadway*. The show goes to Europe. Then, after five months, she gets a job in a new show, *Synchronicity*. This show goes to Japan.

In 1991, Jennifer is back in the US. She is a very good dancer now and she is beautiful, too. A lot of famous singers want the young dancer for their short music movies. Jennifer dances behind the singer Janet Jackson. This helps her and she meets important people in the movie business.

There are no problems with her family now. She has work and she is a success. She has a boyfriend, too— David Cruz.

Later that year, Jennifer moves to Los Angeles for the famous TV show *In Living Color*. Jennifer is a dancer in the show but she is not always happy in her job. She wants to be an actress.

Jennifer the Actress

The head of the TV show *South Central* likes Jennifer's work. In 1993, he wants an actress for the show. He gives the job to Jennifer.

After *South Central*, Jennifer works in three new TV shows: *Second Chances*, *Malibu Road*, and *Nurses on the Line: The Crash of Flight 7*.

Jennifer is now a famous TV star. Then, in 1995, she is in her first Hollywood movie: *Mi Familia*. *Mi Familia* is a "Latin" movie. Her first "English" movies are *Money Train* and *Jack*.

In *Money Train*, Jennifer is Grace Santiago, a New York policewoman. Wesley Snipes and Woody Harrelson play two brothers. They work for the police, too. The two men love Grace. The movie is about their problems.

Jack is a funny movie. Robin Williams plays a boy, Jack. People look at Jack and think, "He's not a boy; he's a man." Jennifer plays Jack's teacher.

In her movies, Jennifer is in love stories with famous men. Her boyfriend, David, is unhappy about this and he goes back to New York.

Jennifer is unhappy, too. But then she finds a new boyfriend. His name is Ojani Noa and he is from Cuba. She marries him in 1997.

In the same year, Jennifer is in four movies. The first movie is *Blood and Wine* with two very famous actors— Jack Nicholson and Michael Caine. The movie is about two bad men—Alex Gates and Victor Spanskey. Jennifer is Gabriella, Alex's girlfriend.

After *Blood and Wine*, Jennifer is in the movies

Jennifer plays a New York policewoman in Money Train.

Anaconda, *U-Turn*, and *Selena*. The movies are a success in the US but *Selena* is a success in Latin countries, too.

In *Selena*, Jennifer plays Selena Quintanilla, the famous Mexican singer. It is an unhappy story because the singer's life was very short. Selena's father gives money for the movie. The director is Gregory Nava. Jennifer works on the movie in front of Selena's family. This is difficult. But the family likes Jennifer, and the movie teaches people about their daughter. This makes Jennifer happy because she liked Selena.

Selena is a big success in many countries. Suddenly, Jennifer Lopez is not only a famous name in the US.

The year 1998 arrives. Jennifer is happy but she can't take a vacation. She is in two movies that year: *Out of Sight* and *Antz*.

In *Out of Sight*, Jennifer is Karen Sisco, a policewoman. George Clooney is Jack Foley. Foley takes money from a bank. He gets away from the police and takes Karen with him. The story is about their love.

Antz is a movie for children. We hear Jennifer but we don't see her face.

Men and Movies

Jennifer's 1998 movies are a big success but Ojani isn't happy. He and David have the same problem. They don't like to see Jennifer with men in love stories. Ojani moves away. Later, he and Jennifer divorce. But they meet often and they are good friends.

In 1999, Jennifer has a new boyfriend. His name is

Jennifer plays Selena Quintanilla, the famous Mexican singer.

Sean Coombs. He is a famous black singer.

On December 27, 1999, Sean and Jennifer come out of a dance bar and get in their car. The police stop them. They find a gun in the front of the car. The gun is not Sean's but the police take him away. Jennifer is in the back of the car. It is not her problem. The story is in the newspapers.

Early in 2000, Jennifer stops seeing Sean. In that year she makes the movie *The Cell*. Jennifer plays Catherine Deane, a doctor. Vincent D'Onofrio plays Carl, a bad man. He takes a young girl. But where is she?

In 2001, Jennifer stars in *The Wedding Planner*. This is a funny movie and a love story. Jennifer plays Maria Fiore. Maria falls in love with Steve Edison, a doctor. *The Wedding Planner* is the number one movie of 2001.

In the same year, Jennifer marries Chris Judd, a dancer, but they divorce in August, 2002. Jennifer stars in two thrillers, *Angel Eyes* and *Enough*. Then she is in *Maid in Manhattan*, a love story.

Jennifer starts going out with the actor Ben Affleck. In 2003, they star in the movie *Gigli*. A lot of newspapers don't like the movie but *Gigli* makes money.

"Are Ben and Jennifer going to marry?" people ask.

The answer is no. Jennifer's love story finishes in September. But in 2004, Ben and Jennifer act in *Jersey Girl*, the story of a father and his little girl. Jennifer is not the star of that movie.

After *Jersey Girl* comes *Shall We Dance?* with Richard Gere. It is a love story about a dance teacher and her student. Jennifer sings for it with her friend Marc Anthony.

Jennifer and Marc sing in Puerto Rico.

Some people are unhappy about Jennifer's movies at this time. "Jennifer doesn't act well and the stories aren't interesting," they say. But 2004 is a good year for Jennifer. She falls in love with Marc.

Jennifer and Marc marry and they are very happy. After the movies *Monster-in-Law*, *An Unfinished Life*, and *Bordertown*, Jennifer and Marc star in *El Cantante*. Marc plays the famous Puerto Rican singer, Héctor Lavoe. Lavoe married Puchi, and Jennifer plays her.

Jennifer the Singer

Music was always important to Jennifer. Today, the famous actress is a famous singer, too.

Jennifer's music success story starts in 1999. In that year, she makes *On the 6*. It is her first music CD. The name comes from the number of a train. Young Jennifer went "on the 6" from a station near her home in New York. On the CD she sings "No Me Ames" with Marc Anthony. She sings in English, too, but the music is Latin. After only five weeks, "If You Had My Love," from the same CD, is number one in the US.

The success of Jennifer the singer doesn't stop. In 2001, her CD *J-Lo* is again number one in the US. She is the first singer–actress with a CD and a movie (*The Wedding Planner*) at number one in the same week.

In 2002, Jennifer makes two music CDs. The first CD of that year is *J to tha L-O! The Remixes*. It gets to number one, too. After that, *This Is Me . . . Then* gets to number two.

Jennifer's CD *Rebirth* arrives in 2005. It gets to number two in the US. Then Jennifer makes her CD *Como Ama Una Mujer*. It is in Spanish. A lot of Latin people love this CD and it is number one in Mexico.

In September, 2007, Jennifer's CD *Brave* arrives. It doesn't have the same success and only gets to number 12 in the US.

Success in Business

Jennifer Lopez is not only an actress. She is not only a dancer, and she is not only a singer. She has success in the fashion business, too.

This starts in 2001. After the success of *The Wedding Planner*, Jennifer opens a clothes business with Andy Hilfiger. Andy is the brother of fashion's famous Tommy Hilfiger. They call their business Sweetface. There aren't many clothes for big women, but this isn't a problem with Sweetface. Jennifer starts JLO, too. From JLO, women can buy clothes, and perfume, too. In a very short time, Jennifer's clothes are famous and her perfume, *Glow*, is number one.

But some people are angry about Jennifer's business. "Some of her clothes come from dead animals," they say. "That's not right."

Jennifer listens because she likes animals. Today, those people are happy.

Jennifer is in the food business, too. In April, 2002, she opens a place in Pasadena, California. Jennifer calls it *Madre's*. *Madre* is "mother" in Spanish. The food there is the Cuban food of her mother's family.

Jennifer's clothes business is a success.

For the Children

Children are important to Jennifer. She does a lot of charity work for sick children and she helps families with very little money. These are important to Marc, too. Today, Jennifer Lopez and Marc Anthony are famous for their charity work.

One night in May, 2007, the two stars are in New York with the famous singer Paul Simon. They ask people for money for sick children. The night is a big success. People give a lot of money to the charity.

And now Jennifer and Marc have children, too. Jennifer's friends and family are very happy for them. For Jennifer, children are very important. This time is important, too. It is a quiet time. For now, work comes after family.

Jennifer Lopez: The Star with Many Faces

She is a dancer, a singer, an actress, a businesswoman, and she helps unhappy children and families. Jennifer Lopez does all of these jobs very well.

In the 1990s, Jennifer Lopez was the number one actress and dancer in the US. Today, she is famous for many things in many countries.

From Asia to America people ask, "Who is our number one Latina?" The answer is always the same:

"Jennifer Lopez, of course."

Jennifer Lopez is a star.

ACTIVITIES

Pages 1–9

Before you read

1 What do you know about Jennifer Lopez? Why is she famous?

2 Look at the photos in the book. What can you see? What do they teach you about Jennifer?

While you read

3 Who:

a	wants to see Jennifer in a good job?	....
b	walks out of the house?	....
c	is Jack?	....
d	is unhappy and goes back to New York?	....
e	is the director of *Selena*?	....
f	has a gun in a car?	....

After you read

4 Work with a friend.

    a *Student A*: You are David Cruz, Jennifer's first boyfriend. Answer the newspaper's questions.

        Student B: You work for a newspaper. Ask David about Jennifer's work. Why is he unhappy about it?

    b Write a "goodbye" letter from David to Jennifer.

Pages 10–14

Before you read

5 Look at the picture on page 12.

    a What do you think of Jennifer's fashions?

    b Which women's clothes do you like?

6 What do you know about:

    a Jennifer the singer?

    b Jennifer the businesswoman?

    c Jennifer and children?

While you read

7 Finish the sentences. Write one word.

    a In 2004, Jennifer and Marc fall in ....

    b *On the 6* is about a ....

    c *J-Lo* and *The Wedding Planner* are number one in the .... week.

    d At *Madre's*, you can eat .... food.

    e Jennifer gives money for .... children.

After you read

8 Who do you like? Jennifer the singer, Jennifer the actress, or Jennifer the businesswoman? Why? Talk to your friends about it.

9 Write about two of these people. Why are they important to Jennifer?

    Guadalupe   Andy Hilfiger   David Cruz

    Selena   Marc Anthony   Janet Jackson

10 Write to Jennifer about an important problem in your country. How can she help?

March 10, 2_ _ _

Dear Ms. Lopez,

Yours sincerely,